VANISHING

GRACE

STUDY GUIDE

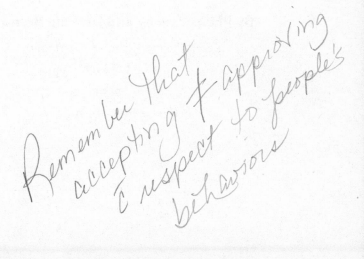

Also by Philip Yancey

By Philip Yancey and Dr. Paul Brand

PHILIP YANCEY

WITH STEPHEN AND AMANDA SORENSON

VANISHING
GRACE

WHAT EVER HAPPENED TO
THE GOOD NEWS?

ZONDERVAN

Vanishing Grace Study Guide
Copyright © 2014 by Philip Yancey

This title is also available as a Zondervan ebook. Visit www.zondervan.com/ebooks.

Requests for information should be addressed to:

Zondervan, 3900 *Sparks Dr. SE, Grand Rapids, Michigan* 49546

ISBN 978-0-310-82549-4

Cover design: Belinda Bass
Cover photography: Chris Hackett/Getty Images (front);
Potapov Alexander/Shutterstock (back)
Interior design: Katherine Lloyd/The DESK

Second Printing February 2015 / Printed in the United States of America

CONTENTS

PREFACE

As a Christian, I have deep concern about how we represent our faith to others. We are called to proclaim the good news of forgiveness and hope, yet I keep coming across evidence that many people do not hear our message as good news. Surveys show that outsiders increasingly view Christians as bearers of bad news, not good news. It appears the church is failing in its mission to dispense God's amazing grace to a world that is thirsty for it.

The journalist in me felt compelled to explore how and why the climate of our culture has taken a dramatically hostile turn against the Christian faith in a very short time. As a committed Christian, I wanted to discover what adjustments we might need to make in order to communicate the good news to our friends, neighbors, coworkers.

So I took a step back to reconsider why the gospel truly is good news to people in our world. I explored the ways Christians seek to engage in a diverse world and discovered that some of our efforts can actually drown out the good news and become stumbling blocks to faith. I also looked for models of people from all walks of life—pilgrims, activists, artists—who are effectively communicating the good news to a culture that is running away from faith.

Grace happens at unexpected moments. It stops us short, catches our breath, disarms us. If we manipulate it, try to control it, or earn it, it is not grace. God's desire is for those of us who have drunk deeply of his grace to offer its healing balm in a world of division and discord. What can we do to show that grace is real, that we can believe in it? How can we lift the cup of amazing grace to the lips of those who have not yet tasted it?

—Philip Yancey,
Spring 2014

HOW TO USE THIS GUIDE

GROUP SIZE

The *Vanishing Grace* video-based curriculum is designed to be experienced in a group setting such as a Bible study, Sunday school class, or any small group gathering. To ensure everyone has enough time to participate in discussions, it is recommended that large groups break up into smaller groups of four to six people each.

MATERIALS NEEDED

Each participant should have his or her own study guide, which includes notes for the five video segments, activities, and discussion questions, as well as personal studies to deepen learning between sessions. Although the course can be fully experienced with just the video and study guide, participants are also encouraged to have a copy of the *Vanishing Grace* book. Reading the book along with the video sessions provides even deeper insights that make the journey richer and more meaningful.

TIMING

The time notations — for example (20 minutes) — indicate the *actual* time of video segments and the *suggested* times for each activity or discussion. Adhering to the suggested times will enable you to complete each session in one hour. Because more discussion questions are provided than most groups can likely get through in an hour-long meeting, feel free to choose in advance the ones you want to be sure to cover. Of course, if you have additional time, you may wish to allow more time for discussion and activities.

FACILITATION

Each group should appoint a facilitator who is responsible for starting the video and for keeping track of time during discussions and activities. Facilitators may also read questions aloud and monitor discussions, prompting participants to respond and ensuring that everyone has the opportunity to participate.

PERSONAL STUDIES

Maximize the impact of the course with between-sessions personal study, which includes both Bible discovery and ways to put that discovery into action.

WE'VE GOT PROBLEMS

Most people I meet assume that Christian means very con-
servative, entrenched in their thinking, anti-gay, anti-choice,
angry, violent, illogical, empire builders; they want to convert
everyone, and they generally cannot live peacefully with anyone
who doesn't believe what they believe.

−UNNAMED CRITIC [1]

INTRODUCTION (8 MINUTES)

As much as Christians may want others to know the good news of forgiveness and experience the hope of a redeemed life, the good news isn't sounding so good to many people these days. In fact, to some "outsiders" the very word *Christian* arouses feelings of fear, distrust, antagonism, and hostility. It is a challenge to be salt and light to people who view Christians so negatively.

Questions to Think About

Choose from among these icebreaker questions as time permits.

1. What experiences have you had with people who react negatively or suspiciously when they find out you are a Christian? If you have had such experiences, share them with the group and discuss how you feel when you interact with those people.

2. If you do not identify yourself as a Christian, what kind of reactions do you get from people who call themselves Christians, and how accepted and valued do you feel by them? (Or, share what non-Christians have told you about whether or not they feel accepted by Christians.)

3. When you engage with someone whose religious, social, or political views differ from yours, to what extent do you think that person feels accepted and valued by you? Share any experiences you may have had when bad feelings resulted from discussions on controversial subjects such as religion or politics.

What kind of attitudes, words, or behaviors might contribute to a person feeling judged or disrespected by you or someone else?

What specific things can you do in an effort to help people whose views differ from yours to still feel accepted and valued by you?

GROUP DISCOVERY (46 MINUTES)

Video Presentation (20 minutes)

Watch the video segment for Session 1, using the following outline to take notes on anything that stands out to you.

Notes

"Nones" who claim no religious faith commitment

A changing climate for the Christian faith

God is good news for:
Individuals

Communities

Societies

The bad news about communicating the good news

Video Discussion (6 minutes)

> *Jesus had the uncanny ability to look at everyone with grace-tinted eyes, seeing not only the beauty of who they were but also the sacred potential of what they could become. We his followers have the same challenge: "So from now on we regard no one from a worldly point of view," Paul told the Corinthians. Evidently we are not doing likewise since many people think of faith, especially evangelical faith, as bad news. They believe Christians view them through eyes of judgment, not eyes of grace. Somehow we need to reclaim the "goodnewsness" of the gospel.*
>
> —*VANISHING GRACE*, PAGE 70

1. How do you respond to the research on the number of "nones" and their increasingly unfavorable impression of Christians? To what degree have you found these trends to be true in your own interaction with people, particularly among the young?

2. What do you think may be the reasons some people perceive the good news of the gospel as bad news?

3. If you asked the question "What's the first thing that comes to your mind when I say the word *Christian*?" what kind of responses might you expect to receive from your acquaintances—coworkers, neighbors, people you meet at a party?

4. What insights into the minds and hearts of people who are not Christians did you discover from Gabe Lyons's observations?

5. If you came to faith a bit later in life, please describe to the group your previous perceptions of and feelings toward Christians and Christianity.

Bible Exploration (15 minutes)

Jesus: Our Model of Grace

The issue is not whether I agree with someone but rather how I treat someone with whom I profoundly disagree. We Christians are called to use the "weapons of grace," which means treating even our opponents with love and respect. As usual, Jesus shows the way.

—*VANISHING GRACE*, PAGE 26

During Jesus' day, Samaritans and Jews had much in common, but they didn't get along. Because of their differences, the two groups became isolated and nursed grudges. The Jews even considered the Samaritans to be heretics.

Jesus, in contrast, dispensed grace everywhere he went. He sought out people who were considered to be "lost." He told parables that emphasized the value of what had gone missing—a lost coin, a wandering lamb, a wayward son. He earnestly desired that all people have the opportunity to hear the gospel — good news about God's love for us, God's forgiveness offered to us, and God's invitation to join his family.

Jesus showed us how to use the "weapons of grace" and treat even our opponents with love and respect. His interaction with the Samaritan woman at the well (John 4:1 – 42) demonstrates what it looks like to see others through eyes of grace.

6. The Gospels give us a hint of the intense animosity between Jews and Samaritans during Jesus' day:

- Which terms did the Pharisees use to insult Jesus in John 8:48?

- What did Jesus' disciples suggest when Samaritans did not welcome Jesus into their village? (See Luke 9:51 – 54.)

- How did Jesus respond in this hostile environment? (See Luke 9:55 – 56.)

7. In stark contrast to the prevailing attitudes of religious Jews and Samaritans, consider how Jesus portrayed members of both groups by reading Luke 10:30 – 35.

- Everyone in Jesus' day knew who the Samaritans, rabbis, and Levites were; how they lived; and how they interacted. How much of a stir do you think this parable might have caused among his audience, and why?

- If Jesus told a similar story about people of opposing political, religious, or social views in our own time, which groups might he include? What impact do you think his story might have on you, and on others?

8. John 4:1–42 lets us in on a close-up encounter between Jesus and a Samaritan woman who was keenly aware of the flashpoints between Jews and Samaritans. As you skim this passage, (1) identify the opposing perspectives revealed, (2) consider how the grace-filled eyes of Jesus saw beyond the conflict, and (3) in each instance notice how Jesus presented the truth of the good news to address the longings of her heart.

- Why was it scandalous for a Jewish rabbi to speak to a Samaritan woman in those days? (See John 4:1–9.)

- How quickly did the cultural and religious tensions over whose heritage was greater crop up in their conversation? (See John 4:10–15.)

- The Samaritan woman was no model of moral character. As you read Jesus' conversation with her, what do you learn about God's love and how to extend grace rather than judgment? (See John 4:16–19.)

- The Jews and Samaritans had a longstanding debate regarding who really knew the right path to God. (See John 4:20–26.) What do you learn from Jesus' dialogue about addressing similar debates regarding differences in denominations and religions today?

- What important question about Jesus did his interaction with the Samaritan woman raise — for her and her community — and what impact did it have? (See John 4:28–30, 39–42.)

- What was Jesus' motivation for this interaction? (See John 4:34.)

9. What did you learn from Jesus' encounter with the Samaritan woman about conveying what Paul calls the "incomparable riches" of God's grace in Ephesians 2:7?

Group Discussion (5 minutes)

> *Make every effort to live in peace with all men and to be holy; without holiness no one will see the Lord. See to it that no one misses the grace of God.*
>
> HEBREWS 12:14–15 (NIV 1984)

During his conversation with the Samaritan woman, Jesus had ample opportunity to fuel animosity and create deep wounds — not just between himself and the woman, but between himself and her village, between the people of her village and all Jews. It would have been so easy to put up barriers that cause division. Yet Jesus chose to take down those barriers, to dispense God's grace, to pour out his living water to anyone who was thirsty.

10. Animosity similar to that between the ancient Jews and Samaritans exists between Christians and others today.

   • Identify some of these groups and describe the conflicts that exist.

- How much does the growing public hostility toward Christianity concern you, and to what degree have you felt anxiety or fear over our increasingly "post-Christian" culture?

11. Jesus has granted us, as his followers, the immense privilege of dispensing God's grace to a thirsty world—including the groups identified in question 10. But when we ignore basic principles of relationship by making condescending judgments, proclamations that aren't backed by compassionate action, or speaking without first listening, we fail to love—we fail to communicate grace and thus deter a thirsty world from finding the source of living water.

    - Identify several ways we Christians may be obscuring the view of God's grace for people in our world, giving personal anecdotes if you can.

    - Consider practical changes—in specific attitudes, actions, and words—that we can make to take down those barriers and make God's grace more visible to those who have not experienced it.

- Which agendas (that may be very good and well intentioned) might we need to adjust or even let go of in order to make God's grace more visible?

12. If you feel comfortable doing so, give examples from your experience about ways in which Christians have created deep wounds and hostility—perhaps in the name of God. What have you learned from such negative experiences that may help us to better reach out to those who have been wounded by our failure to dispense God's grace in our world?

PERSONAL REFLECTION (4 MINUTES)

Christians can come across as superior and judgmental, dismissing others' beliefs while being defensive about their own. When I sense those tendencies in myself, I try to remember how I feel when someone argues that I'm wrong about something—which gives a strong clue to how others must feel when I present my own beliefs insensitively. I've yet to meet someone who found their way to faith by being criticized.

VANISHING GRACE, PAGES 43–44

As you reflect on Jesus' interaction with the Samaritan woman, which persons come to mind who, like the woman, long for but have not experienced the life-giving grace of God?

How concerned are you that these persons have not heard the good news in a way they can recognize as a valuable and desirable gift from God, and what might you do to change that?

How might your present attitudes come across to these persons? How might your interactions improve if you were more intentional about:

• Viewing them more as spiritually thirsty rather than as *wrong*?

• Seeking to convey God's good news of forgiveness and hope not just in words but hand-in-hand with sincere, loving action?

• Living in a way that is so significantly different from the norm that even those who disagree with you can't miss the aroma of Christ and are drawn toward faith in God?

• Stepping back from the "us versus them" attitude and becoming more thoughtful and considerate in expressing your opinions and judgments regarding people you disagree with or who don't believe as you believe?

- Responding to criticism or judgment with "a gentle answer" that turns away anger (Proverbs 15:1) as opposed to a hostile, harsh attack that escalates it?

CLOSING PRAYER (2 MINUTES)

Begin your prayer with these words from the Bible:

> *Blessed are you when people insult you, persecute you and falsely say all kinds of evil against you because of me ... You have heard that it was said, "Love your neighbor and hate your enemy." But I tell you, love your enemies and pray for those who persecute you.*
>
> MATTHEW 5:11, 43–44

Continue in prayer, focusing on Jesus, who teaches us to love our enemies, to pray for those who persecute us, and to continue dispensing grace to a hurting, thirsty world. Ask for forgiveness and healing for the ways in which you may have caused people to turn away from, rather than seek, God. Pray that God will break down barriers between you and those who are not Christians, teaching you to be more loving, sensitive, patient, and kind. Ask God to fill you with courage and compassion as you offer his living water to others.

Personal Journey: To Do on Your Own

God didn't go to all the trouble of sending his Son merely to point an accusing finger, telling the world how bad it was. He came to help, to put the world right again.

JOHN 3:17, *THE MESSAGE*

Bible Discovery

Jesus came for the sick and not the well, for sinners and not for saints. Thankfully, many people who are not Christians remain open to faith. They are drawn to the gospel's answers to questions of meaning, its promise of afterlife, and provision of support for those in need.

But Christians today face great challenges when sharing the good news with the growing number of people who have negative impressions of Christianity, who are apathetic, suspicious, or even hostile to the gospel message. Nothing short of an encounter with Jesus' love for those who are lost will set the world right for these men and women.

1. Many of Jesus' stories center on themes of compassion, longing, and sacrifice for what is lost. Read the parables of the lost coin and lost sheep in Luke 15:4–10.

   • What do these parables reveal about the priority Jesus places on reaching spiritually lost people?

- What is the motivation for finding that which is lost—scolding or saving?

- What is the response when the lost are found?

- To what degree does your motivation for engaging "the lost" reflect that of Jesus?

2. In 2 Corinthians 5:14–20 Paul wrote, "For Christ's love compels us … So from now on we regard no one from a worldly point of view. Though we once regarded Christ in this way, we do so no longer … All this is from God, who reconciled us to himself through Christ and gave us the ministry of reconciliation: that God was reconciling the world to himself in Christ, not counting people's sins against them. And he has committed to us the message of reconciliation. We are therefore Christ's ambassadors, as though God were making his appeal through us."

   - When it comes to interacting with people with whom we disagree, how would you describe the "worldly point of view" and its result?

- In contrast, what do you think is God's point of view on people who oppose the good news and its messengers?

- In light of this passage, write out for yourself what it means to "regard no one from a worldly point of view" and to be an ambassador of reconciliation between God and those who do not know (and may vehemently oppose) God.

Take Action

1. In what ways has my perspective on how to relate to people who are not Christians changed as a result of this session?

2. Who in my circle of influence do I now see as a lost, spiritually *thirsty* person who longs for meaning and fulfillment rather than as someone I'm tempted to judge—or even as an enemy?

How do I want to treat this person differently when we interact in the future?

3. What do I think attracted those people who were frowned upon by most religious types to Jesus?

Which of these characteristics of Jesus do I want to cultivate in order to better live out my faith in a thirsty and sometimes hostile world?

4. What one step will I take to tone down any animosity I feel toward people who are hostile toward Christianity and bring them God's healing grace instead?

WHAT CAN WE DO ABOUT IT?

A new command I give you: Love one another. As I have loved you, so you must love one another. By this everyone will know that you are my disciples, if you love one another.

—JOHN 13:34 – 35

INTRODUCTION (8 MINUTES)

The British writer Theodore Dalrymple confesses, "It is not as easy as one might suppose to rid oneself of the notion of God."[2] Apparently believing that there is no God or simply ignoring the possibility doesn't make the thirst go away. Despite the allure of entertainment and material goods, modern people feel a void. We long for meaning, a sense that our life matters. We long for community, a sense of being loved. Surely there must be a better way for Christians to display the grace of God—to draw others to the faith rather than to repel them.

Questions to Think About

Choose from among these icebreaker questions as time permits.

1. How do you respond when you feel a person does not have your best interests at heart or is trying to push an agenda on you? Relate a specific example, if you can.

   What tips you off to the person's true motivation?

   As you consider the way Christians interact with people who are not Christians, what attitudes, words, or actions might reveal a self-serving motivation rather than a motivation of love for that person?

2. What difference does it make if you respond with grace, respect, and kindness to someone who angrily opposes you and your beliefs about God and the Bible?

3. What are some attitudes, words, or actions that have the potential to reach through the defenses of a non-Christian and make a positive, "good news" impact?

GROUP DISCOVERY (47 MINUTES)

Video Presentation (20 minutes)

Watch the video segment for Session 2, using the following outline to take notes on anything that stands out to you.

Notes

Commanded to love

Showing God's grace to those who oppose us

Loving even our enemies as God loves them

Reaching out to those around us by:

Awakening their spiritual thirst

Being present during their hinge moments

Video Discussion (5 minutes)

Jesus set forth love as the essence of what we are supposed to be about: to love God with all our heart, soul, and mind, and to love our neighbors as we love ourselves. If our primary motivation is love, that cuts through defenses. Love means I listen to someone, identify with their need or perhaps their pain, and truly care for them—whether or not they show any interest in my faith. Without love, nothing else we do really matters, no matter how impressive, spiritual, or well intentioned it may be.

FROM THE *VANISHING GRACE* VIDEO

1. How well do you think we Christians are doing in our current efforts to engage culture and share the good news with those who do not know or desire it?

2. What have you observed about attempts by Christians to connect with people on a spiritual level in a "post-Christian" environment?

   What have these experiences taught you about how we might share the good news more effectively?

3. Consider how Christopher Hitchens, a strident atheist, responded to the grace Dr. Collins extended to him.

   Would you consider Dr. Collins to be "successful" in extending God's grace and proclaiming the good news to Christopher Hitchens? Why or why not?

How do you feel about the fact that Hitchens perhaps never became a Christian despite Dr. Collins's efforts?

4. Do you think the couple who loved Rosaria Butterfield was more "successful" in sharing the good news with her than Dr. Collins was with Christopher Hitchens? Why or why not?

5. What do you think might be at the root of the urge to "push" our beliefs on people, trying to change their beliefs, rather than dropping our agendas and simply loving them so that they experience the love and good news of Jesus?

Bible Exploration (17 minutes)

The Good News: God's Message of Love

It takes no grace to relate to someone who looks, thinks, and acts just like me ... The more we love, and the more unlikely people we love, the more we resemble God—who, after all, loves ornery creatures like us.

VANISHING GRACE, PAGES 37, 39

God has a large stake in how we love. While it is unlikely that God keeps track of how many arguments we win, God may indeed keep track of how well we love. Why is our love for others so important to God? First John 4:12 explains that love is how we make known an invisible God: "No one has ever seen God; but if we love one another, God lives in us and his love is made complete in us." So love is the indispensable starting point to presenting faith in a grace-full way. The core problem with communicating our faith today is that we do not always do so in love.

6. What did Jesus say would set Christians apart from other people, and how well are we following that command today? (See John 13:34–35.)

7. In a command found in no other religion, what does Jesus tell us to do? (See Matthew 5:43–44.)

How well do we do this?

How might we encourage and help one another to do this more faithfully?

8. What is God's standard for loving the unlovely? (See Luke 6:31–36.)

Why is this important?

How might such an attitude of heart and mind guide us in sharing God's message of love and good news?

9. Many Christians recognize 1 Corinthians 13 as the Bible's "love chapter." We may even be able to recite it. But putting its message into practice is quite another matter. Read verses 1–7 aloud, considering how Paul's message applies to the way we share the good news with spiritually thirsty people.

• In our human efforts to "set things right" in the world, it is easy to become overzealous in action (even good action) and to overlook love, which should be the foundation for all we do. In contrast, how highly does Paul value the way of love (v. 1)?

- What examples of Christians congratulating ourselves for triumphing over those who oppose us can you think of? (Remember, these are the same people with whom we are to share the good news!) What can we learn from this passage about the proper balance between standing against evil in the culture and loving individual people?

- According to this passage, when we act or speak without love, what do we produce? And to what extent might we deserve some of the unpleasant words people use to describe Christians?

- What does love always do (v. 7), and what impact will these actions have on our relationships and interaction with those who do not acknowledge God?

10. The parable of the prodigal son, who rejected the values of his family and the life of faith, portrays the depth of God's love for those who are lost. It also challenges the faithful to test the purity of our love for the lost. Read this parable together, from Luke 15:11–32.

   • How influential is this story in opening our hearts to truly love the lost — not just want them "saved" but *love* them?

   • To what extent does this story open our hearts to love those who have rejected God — those we might identify as post-Christian?

   • Consider again verses 17–20. What did the son eventually realize about his father that led him home, and how might this be like or unlike the way you impact a lost person's heart and life?

• Note the family tension that arose when the father began to celebrate his wayward son's return (vv. 22–32). What might keep us from eagerly celebrating the homecoming of those who have been lost, and what changes of heart and practice might we need to make in response?

Group Discussion (5 minutes)

The uncommitted share many of our core values, but if we do not live out those values in a compelling way, we will not awaken their thirst for their ultimate Source. Christians can do no better than to follow the example set by Jesus, who specialized not in techniques and arguments but in spirit and example. He took skeptics seriously, listening to them and responding forthrightly and yet compassionately.

VANISHING GRACE, PAGE 59

11. It makes a huge difference whether we treat nonbelievers as *wrong* or as individuals who are on the way but lost. In the cultural center of Athens, the apostle Paul encountered suspicion, curiosity, hostility, and ridicule. Rather than condemning the Athenians to hell, he built his case for Christ from common ground. Notice some of the phrases he used (Acts 17:22–28): "I see that in every way you are very religious," "I walked around and looked carefully at your objects of worship," "the very thing you worship … I am going to proclaim to you," "God who made the world … does not live in temples built by human hands … God did this so that they would seek him … reach out for him … find him, though he is not far from any one of us."

- What did Paul say that demonstrated humble and loving respect, and what might we say to communicate the same grace to people in our world?

- What did Paul do that shows he truly cared about the people of Athens and what they valued? In what specific ways might we need to "get out and walk around" in order to better know, understand, and express sincere love for people we encounter?

- Notice how Paul expressed what he had in common with his audience. What do we have in common with people who are not Christians, and how might that common ground become a bridge to future spiritual interaction?

12. Atticus Finch, the fictional lawyer in *To Kill a Mockingbird*, said, "You never really understand a person until you consider things from his point of view ... until you climb into his skin and walk about in it."[3]

- Think of people you know who are not believers. What do you think climbing into their skin and walking about in it might look like? Be as specific as you can.

- Why do you think it is necessary to immerse ourselves in another person's point of view, and what makes it so hard to do?

- How might our stereotypes of non-Christians hinder us from truly understanding their point of view?

13. The video portion of this session concluded with examples of several people who found unique opportunities to help others experience something of the grace of God—a Christian Internet wedding pastor, a Southern Baptist pastor who operates a private cigar club, a woman who treats telemarketers with compassion and grace. What other ideas does your group have for expressing God's grace to those who are lost and thirsty?

PERSONAL REFLECTION (3 MINUTES)

*Do nothing out of selfish ambition or vain conceit.
Rather, in humility value others above yourselves, not
looking to your own interests but each of you to the interests of others. In your relationships with one another,
have the same mindset as Christ Jesus: Who, being in
very nature God, did not consider equality with God
something to be used to his own advantage.*

PHILIPPIANS 2:3–6

As Christians, we sometimes become self-focused and complacent,
satisfied to know and talk about the good news but unwilling to
live it out for the benefit of those who don't know it. During this
session, you've been encouraged to recognize the importance of living out love through grace-full actions that display the good news
of the gospel. You've been invited to build caring, sincere relationships with spiritually thirsty people and to be sensitive to the "hinge
moments" when the good news of Jesus may be heard. Now it's time
to consider how to do it.

During the tough times of life, many of us—non-Christian and
Christian alike—find ourselves spiritually hungry and thirsty. We
long to fill the nagging void in our souls.

During the difficult times of your life, who cared enough to
step in and help fill that need in your soul?

Which of that person's characteristics, words, and actions
were most helpful and meaningful to you?

What impact did that person's outpouring of love have on your understanding of God or your relationship with God?

Which characteristics do you now realize are important to model as you interact with people during the hinge moments of their lives, and why are they important?

What changes do you need to make so that you become more aware of the hinge moments in people's lives and more available to reach out to them during those times?

CLOSING PRAYER (2 MINUTES)

Begin your prayer with these words from the Bible:

> *Live such good lives among the pagans that, though they accuse you of doing wrong, they may see your good deeds and glorify God on the day he visits us.*
>
> I PETER 2:12

Continue in prayer, confessing your failure to fully live the good life of love and grace that God desires. Renew your desire and commitment to express God's love to people around you. Ask God to give you the heart to show grace to those who are hostile to you as well as to those who may recognize their spiritual thirst. Thank God for every opportunity to dispense grace.

Personal Journey: To Do on Your Own

*Love the Lord your God with all your heart and with
all your soul and with all your mind and with all your
strength ... Love your neighbor as yourself.*

MARK 12:30–31

Bible Discovery

We truly have no greater privilege in life than to love God and
to share the good news of God's love with everyone we encounter. Sometimes the good news will connect in a powerful way with
people who recognize their spiritual thirst. Other times, it will be
greeted with hostility. In either case, God loves wayward children
and wants each one to be restored to the family. It is up to us to live
out God's love in a compelling way — to so overflow with grace and
love that the thirst of the lost is awakened and satisfied.

1. Barbara Brown Taylor remembers well her own wanderings
   in life. She says that the unexpected turns remind her "that
   God does some of God's best work with people who are truly,
   seriously lost."[4] While he was on earth, Jesus spent time with
   people of his day who qualified as "truly, seriously lost." What
   impact did his love have on people we might dismiss as being
   hopelessly beyond reach? (See Matthew 9:10–12; 26:6–13;
   Luke 7:37–38; 19:2–10.)

   • What do you take to heart from these examples about
     dispensing grace to the seriously lost?

- How eager are the seriously lost—including the needy, sick, atheist, dispossessed, vulnerable—to spend time with us, and what do you think this reveals about our love for them?

- What can we do to make it easier for lost people whose spiritual beliefs and values may differ significantly from ours to feel loved and welcome to participate in our day-to-day lives?

2. The Bible records numerous examples of people who were thirsty to satisfy their deep longings. As you read about these individuals, consider whether their longing was physical, spiritual, social, or emotional, and identify similar longings in people in your world. Also, consider how the longing was satisfied (if it was) and how you might share the love and grace of God when you encounter people who have similar longings.

   - Bartimaeus (Mark 10:46–52)

- Nicodemus (John 3:1–9)

- Herod (Mark 6:17–20)

- A rich young man (Matthew 19:16–22)

- Ethiopian eunuch (Acts 8:26–35)

- Thief on the cross (Luke 23:39–42)

Take Action

A restless search for pleasure, fear of death, boredom, addiction—any of these can betray a longing that is at root spiritual, the cries and whispers of someone who has lost the way.

What other symptoms of spiritual thirst would I add to this list?

Which specific longings have I seen expressed in people around me, and how willing and prepared am I to bring love, grace, and hope into that person's world? What changes and complications might that require in my life?

What practical steps can I take in order to become more sensitive and responsive to the longings of people I encounter?

A hospital chaplain provides helpful insights for how to bring genuine compassion and comfort to hurting people, including those who are not Christians. Use these insights (see next page) as a starting point for helping people you know to experience something of the grace of God in the midst of their struggles and unmet longings. Take note of why each insight is important for where the person is at this point in time. Then pray for opportunities, wisdom, and grace to love that person as God would love him or her.

Insights	Why this is important as I reach out in love to _____:
Remember, God is already present with you	
The person has a story I can learn from	
Show attentive respect	
Maintain good eye contact	
Convey a sense of ease, not cockiness	
Let the person determine the conversation's direction	
Prayers should express love and compassion, not a veiled message	

Take a few moments right now to ask God to guide you in responding appropriately during "hinge moment" opportunities in people's lives. Ask God to help you find common ground and cultivate friendships based on respect and genuine love.

WHO ARE THE GRACE DISPENSERS?

Each of you should use whatever gift you have received to serve others, as faithful stewards of God's grace in its various forms. If anyone speaks, they should do so as one who speaks the very words of God. If anyone serves, they should do so with the strength God provides, so that in all things God may be praised through Jesus Christ. To him be the glory and the power for ever and ever. Amen.

—1 PETER 4:10 – 11

INTRODUCTION (8 MINUTES)

Although many nonbelievers are not opposed to spiritual search-ing, they are growing increasingly suspicious of and hostile toward spirituality that bears the name *Christian*. They often close their ears to the words of the evangelist and argue against the apologist. If the uncommitted don't want to hear about or investigate the claims of the good news, how can we possibly communicate it to them?

Questions to Think About

Choose from among these icebreaker questions as time permits.

1. We know that Jesus designated his followers to be dispens-ers of grace, his messengers of good news in a thirsty world. What results do we expect as we seek to share his grace in the world? What happens to our hope and expectations when the task is difficult or seemingly fruitless?

2. How do you feel when someone seems resistant or even hostile toward the life-giving gift of God's love and mercy?

3. Based on your experience, which groups of Christians are more effective than others in communicating the good news to people who have little to do with God or the church? What are they doing that differs from the norm? Why do you think it makes a difference?

GROUP DISCOVERY (47 MINUTES)

Video Presentation (20 minutes)

Watch the video segment for Session 3, using the following outline to take notes on anything that stands out to you.

Notes

Those who dispense grace well
    Activists: demonstrating faith with their hands

       Artists: bypassing the head to speak gently to the heart

Pilgrims: ordinary followers of Jesus who come alongside to point the way

Video Discussion (5 minutes)

While discussing the growing antipathy toward Christians, a friend remarked, "There are three kinds of Christians that outsiders to the faith still respect: pilgrims, activists, and artists. The uncommitted will listen to them far sooner than to an evangelist or apologist." [5] *They will listen only to those Christians who present themselves as fellow-pilgrims on the way rather than as part of a superior class who has already arrived. Activists express their faith in the most persuasive way of all, by their deeds. And art succeeds when it speaks most authentically to the human condition; when believers do so with skill, again the world takes note.*

VANISHING GRACE, PAGE 89

1. If you have had the impression that there is only one way to share the good news and you're not cut out to do it well, what does the concept of *artist*, *activist*, and *pilgrim* grace dispensers mean to you?

2. In what way did Holly's and Makoto's interviews encourage you or inspire new ideas and avenues for living out and sharing your faith? How could you put their ideas into practice in your own life?

3. Consider for a moment the people who have touched your life. Which of the three types of grace dispensers—activist, artist, or pilgrim—influenced your walk of faith the most?

What was it about that person's presence, message, or deeds that cut through your defenses and communicated God's grace to you?

In what ways has that person's example opened up possibilities for you to extend God's gift of grace to others, particularly to those who might be perceived as difficult to reach?

4. What is the one kind of grace dispenser that every follower of Jesus can be despite our skills, mistakes, doubts, and failures?

5. What would you say makes grace compelling when it is offered by an artist? By an activist? By a pilgrim?

Bible Exploration (15 minutes)

Being Grace Dispensers

He [Jesus] went to Nazareth, where he had been brought up, and on the Sabbath day he went into the synagogue, as was his custom. He stood up to read, and the scroll of the prophet Isaiah was handed to him. Unrolling it, he found the place where it is written: "The Spirit of the Lord is on me, because he has anointed me to proclaim good news to the poor. He has sent me to proclaim freedom for the prisoners and recovery of sight for the blind, to set the oppressed free."

LUKE 4:16–18

Jesus came bearing good news. Everywhere he went, Jesus dispensed God's grace in abundance — teaching, healing, feeding, delivering; restoring life and hope. Before ascending to heaven, Jesus commissioned his followers to continue his work by proclaiming that good news in every corner of the earth. In a world that desperately needs the glad tidings of God's love, it is a bit intimidating to realize that we bumbling pilgrims are "the Jesus left behind." We are the ones called to use our God-given talents and gifts to bear witness of God's kingdom, to share the greatest news ever known.

6. Read Matthew 25:34–40, where Jesus tells a story that draws attention to the needs of the whole person, not just the soul.

- Sometimes Christians who communicate their faith focus our gospel witness on just one part of life — or perhaps the afterlife — rather than the whole person. What examples of this can you think of, and what has been the result?

- Why do you think the truth of God's love and forgiveness has a greater impact when we minister to the whole person?

- When we reach out to people in need — the hungry, sick, imprisoned, homeless — who does Jesus say we are really serving, and why is this important to remember?

7. When those of us who follow Jesus display God's grace by caring for vulnerable and needy people, what message about God are we sending to a skeptical world? (See Matthew 5:14–16; 1 John 3:16–18.)

Why do you think communicating in this way—through a visible apologetic—is important for people who are suspicious of or completely reject the good news of God's grace?

What do you think skeptical people long to see in us and our message?

8. Gina Welch, whose story is told in *Vanishing Grace,* was an "outsider" to the Christian faith who immersed herself in an evangelical church for the purpose of investigative research. As she got to know Christians, she found them to be less like members of a private club for the righteous and more like people with the same struggles as everyone else she knew. In that community of pilgrims she discovered transformed lives, got to know people who gladly paid a significant personal cost to live out their values, and found a safe place where people could share their struggles and reset their moral compass. As you read the following Bible passages, take note of the grace Jesus' followers are blessed to experience that can be good news for people who do not know God.

Bible Passage(s)	The Message of Grace We Have to Share
Ephesians 1:7; 1 John 1:9	
2 Thessalonians 2:16–17; Hebrews 4:15–16; 2 Peter 1:3–4	
Romans 3:22–24; Ephesians 2:4–9; 2 Timothy 1:8–9; Titus 2:11–14	
Ephesians 3:7–8	
2 Corinthians 9:8	
1 Peter 4:10	
Hebrews 12:1–3	
Colossians 4:6	

9. Pilgrims live out their faith best in community with other pilgrims. Wayne Hoag, a pastor in California, did a series of sermons on twenty-nine uses of the phrase "one another" in the New Testament, which, taken together, show what a true pilgrim community would look like. Read the following selection of "one another" phrases and discuss how such an emphasis might play out in your church or spiritual community. What would this style of relating require of us? What kind of community would it build? Why might such a community tend to attract, rather than repel, the world around us? What examples can you give of believers who practice such principles?

Bible Passage	How Jesus Followers Are to Relate to One Another
John 13:34–35	Love one another
Romans 12:10	Be devoted to one another; honor one another
Romans 14:13	Stop passing judgment on one another
Romans 15:7	Accept one another
Ephesians 4:32	Be kind and compassionate to one another
1 Thessalonians 5:11	Encourage and build up one another
Hebrews 10:24	Spur one another on to love and good deeds
Colossians 3:13	Forgive one another
James 5:16	Pray for each other
Galatians 6:2	Carry one another's burdens
2 Corinthians 1:3–4	Comfort one another with the comfort we have received
Romans 12:16–18	Live in harmony with one another

10. What main thing did Jesus pray for the community he would leave behind? Why is this important as we strive to be "stewards of God's grace," or grace dispensers, in the world? (See John 17:11, 20–21.)

Group Discussion (7 minutes)

> *Christians are not mere wayfarers en route to the next life, but rather pioneers of God's kingdom in advance, a sign of what will follow. By living out lives of grace in a spoiled environment, we point forward to a time of restoration.*
>
> VANISHING GRACE, PAGES 129–130

11. What impact do you think Jesus followers would have on spiritually uncommitted people if we—pilgrims, activists, artists, all united as a church community—carried out Paul's charge in Philippians: "Go out into the world uncorrupted, a breath of fresh air in this squalid and polluted society. Provide people with a glimpse of good living and of the living God" (Philippians 2:14–16, *The Message*)?

What opportunities exist in your community to bring the fresh air of grace to a "squalid and polluted society"? (For example, ministering in prisons, clinics, childcare centers, or schools; promoting justice; offering job training; advocating for the exploited; coming alongside victims of disasters.)

What practical gifts of God's grace do you have to offer individually and as a group?

In what ways might the Christian community do a better job of supporting activists who touch human needs with the grace of God, and what difference might that support make?

12. Why do you think activists' hands-on acts of grace are more palatable — perhaps even impressive — to skeptics and post-Christians, while fervent efforts to intentionally transform the culture or to "change the world for Christ" tend to provoke opposition?

In the long run, are such acts of grace more, or less, effective in changing the world for Christ? Explain your answer.

13. Pastor Rick Warren writes, "I'm looking for a second reformation. The first reformation of the church 500 years ago was about beliefs. This one is going to be about deeds. It is not going to be about what the church believes, but about what the church is doing."[6]

    • What do you think about this statement and its ramifications for our society?

    • If this statement is true, in what ways do you think the church is changing, and will continue to change along this line?

    • If this statement is not true, how can the church do a better job of affecting society for the good?

14. Consider how the arts have become a pulpit for culture at large, and how powerful its impact might be.

   • Would you agree or disagree that people of faith have too often neglected the potential for the arts to communicate to spiritually thirsty people? Why?

   • In our culture, where most "nones" will not set foot inside a church, what potential do you see for encounters with the good news to occur in art museums, movies, plays, books, or concerts? Can you give examples from the arts of powerful presentations of the Christian message?

   • What challenges might people of faith face when they seek to communicate God's grace through the arts?

   • How might we, as a community of Jesus-followers, encourage Christian artists who often work in seclusion behind the frontlines and may struggle to find venues for their creative work to be displayed?

15. Jesus-followers today often have the idea that we must have it all together and have all the right answers before we can share the good news of God's grace. Rather than viewing ourselves as fellow pilgrims on the journey through life, we take on the role of professional guides. What drawbacks do you see to the professional guide role—for the spiritually uncommitted, for you as a grace dispenser, and for the ministry of God's church at large?

Which attitudes and actions can turn off nonbelievers, keeping us from connecting with them in a meaningful way?

Which attitudes and actions add authenticity to the message of God's grace?

If you have friends or relatives who have been helped by the recovery movement or 12-step programs, what have you learned from them about the "pilgrim" approach?

PERSONAL REFLECTION (3 MINUTES)

In some incomprehensible way, we ordinary pilgrims have the capacity to bring parental pride to the God of the universe. The notion fills me with awe and wonder—and sometimes regret. At the end of the day I ask myself, "What did I do to bring God pleasure today?" I review my interactions with neighbors, the way I handled an unwelcome phone call, my use of money and time. Did I "please God in every way" as Paul prayed for the Colossians?

VANISHING GRACE, PAGE 104

For a Jesus-follower, the opportunity to please God is our greatest honor and privilege. One way we bring pleasure to God is by dispensing grace to those who do not know God. For those who have lost their way, we can point to the ultimate Source of love, hope, meaning, and purpose. After all, God wants us to experience the life-changing gift of grace and live the most fulfilled, meaningful life on earth.

What gift do you believe God has given you to dispense God's grace in this world? (Your answer might range from writing music to repairing cars for low-income parents to addressing lawmakers to tutoring disadvantaged children to being a listening ear for a terminally ill—or anything else that occurs to you.)

How do you use this gift to bring pleasure to God every day?

When you look at what is wrong in the world, what are you particularly concerned about?

If you have complained to God about this concern but the problem persists, do you think God may be telling you to start doing something about it yourself? Why or why not?

Do you see your role in being part of God's solution to this situation as that of an activist? An artist? A pilgrim? Something else?

What might be a first step for you to take in bringing God's grace to bear on this situation? And who in your faith community might join you as a co-laborer, a supporter in prayer, or a fellow pilgrim to keep you on track?

CLOSING PRAYER (2 MINUTES)

Begin your prayer with these words from the Bible:

> *And God is able to bless you abundantly, so that in all things at all times, having all that you need, you will abound in every good work. As it is written: "They have freely scattered their gifts to the poor; their righteousness endures forever."*
>
> 2 CORINTHIANS 9:8–9

Continue praying, asking God to guide you in dispensing grace through deed as well as by word. Pray about the talents and gifts God has given you—and how God may desire to use you as a pilgrim, activist, and/or artist. Ask God to give you a heart of love for others and to reveal attitudes and actions that may hinder you from dispensing grace effectively. Thank God for taking pleasure in everything we do for his glory.

Personal Journey: To Do on Your Own

How, then, can they call on the one they have not believed in? And how can they believe in the one of whom they have not heard? And how can they hear without someone preaching to them? And how can anyone preach unless they are sent? As it is written, "How beautiful are the feet of those who bring good news!"

ROMANS 10:14–15

Bible Discovery

Often Christians try to appear to have it all together when we relate to non-Christians. So we come across as controlling people who tell others what to do and how to think rather than as pilgrims on a spiritual journey. The truth is, Jesus called us to be servants, and servants empty themselves of privilege and any sense of superiority. We must not forget that we are needy, forgiven people who dispense God's grace with all our weakness. A jaded world will find it easier to identify with us and hear the good news when we are sincere, authentic, admitting our need for the very grace we seek to share.

1. Read Luke 4:18–19; James 1:27; 2:15–17; 3:17–18.
   What do these passages reveal about how much God wants us to administer grace to needy and vulnerable people?

How do you want to respond to God's desire expressed in these verses?

2. The following verses provide insight into the small band of unreliable disciples (ordinary pilgrims on their spiritual journey) that Jesus chose and empowered to change the world as they lived out and shared the good news of the kingdom of God. Take note of how very human—fallible, honest, committed, bewildered, overjoyed—they were. Yet these same flawed people did indeed change the world! Then consider how God can use you, with your strengths, weaknesses, doubts, successes, failures, and hopes to bring life-changing grace into your world.

Bible Passage	The Ordinary Disciples God Used	The Ordinary Me God Can Use
Matthew 8:24–27		
Matthew 16:5–12		
Matthew 28:16–17		
Mark 9:33–35		

Bible Passage	The Ordinary Disciples God Used	The Ordinary Me God Can Use
Luke 22:54–62		
John 14:8–12		
John 16:16–20		
John 20:19–28		
John 21:1–3		

Take Action

Whether you are an artist, activist, or pilgrim, God is calling every follower of Jesus to dispense grace to a needy world—to share the love and forgiveness we have experienced and the guidance we've received from the Bible. We're not an elite club or superior class. We are simply ordinary people who have found something wonderful to give away. It is up to us to be faithful stewards of God's grace, and every one of us can do it.

Through this session you have gained new perspective on how you, with your unique gifts, can share the gospel with people who are lost. Now let's push the envelope a bit. Although each of us may identify ourselves as one type of grace dispenser, we are not that exclusively. Other opportunities to share God's grace will arise. It may be tempting to turn your back on these moments if they aren't within your comfort zone, but please consider other possibilities you might have to share God's grace.

- Even though I am an **activist**, when in my faith journey have I also been a pilgrim, a person who has to figure things out, makes mistakes, and learns a better way?

  What "pilgrim" opportunities might come before me in my world? For example, during difficult challenges that arise in my arena of activism how might I come alongside another activist who is struggling and share my learning experiences and the hope that sees me through the difficult times?

- As an **artist**, I may sense something like God's "still, small voice." When should I be more direct by tugging at the heart and awakening the Spirit within people? And when should I be more indirect, taking into account their capacity to receive the message?

  In what ways might I take greater risks with my work, pushing against the envelope to incite change or action in people around me? Am I willing to do that? Why or why not?

How might I use my creative work to support activists and pilgrims in dispensing grace?

- I may be a **pilgrim**, but I also recognize that by creating me in his image, God placed a spark of creative artistry within me. I may never sculpt, sing a note on key, or write a moving poem, but as I come alongside and share myself with another person, when might that God-given spark of artistry blossom into a grace-filled moment?

For example, might I read a story with such understanding and expression that a passion for reading and writing is awakened in a child who will become a great communicator of God's love? Or might I recommend a particular book that sparks a lively discussion on faith in a book club or reading group?

Perhaps I am a student of God's artistry in creation—intricate biology, spectacular geology, amazing heavens. Might there be appropriate opportunities to share with skeptics the ways those wonders point me to my glorious Creator?

IS IT REALLY GOOD NEWS?

Without doubt, the church has made grievous errors over the centuries. Despite it all, the kingdom of God continues to grow, bearing the fruit of freedom, dignity, and compassion. We will never create a perfect society; ours certainly needs a lot of help. But in measurable, inarguable ways, the gospel message is good news, bringing hope wherever it is planted.

—FROM THE VANISHING GRACE VIDEO

INTRODUCTION (8 MINUTES)

Certainly our world needs good news. Cultural trends in the U.S. reveal a society that is sliding in the wrong direction. The wonders of science and technology have not satisfied our nagging emptiness. Divorce, teen suicide, violent crime, out-of-wedlock births, and homelessness are all symptoms of society's ills. The leading causes of death are self-inflicted — side effects of tobacco, obesity, alcohol, sexually transmitted disease, drugs, and violence. We need a transformation. We need the kind of personal and societal renewal in which Jesus-followers who bear the good news of God's love and forgiveness could play a crucial role.

Questions to Think About

Choose from among these icebreaker questions as time permits.

1. If you were to ask non-Christians you know what the Christian message is, and whether or not it is good news, how do you think they would answer?

    What about their answers might please you or trouble you?

    Would you expect most people in our society to have similar answers? If so, what might be the implications of their opinions? If not, how might other people respond?

2. "Christianity is nothing but bad news. Think of the Cru-
    sades, the Inquisition, the Moral Majority. Religion is just
    one more way of controlling other people." What do you
    think might be a grace-full way to respond to a person who
    dismisses Christianity in this way?

3. Clearly, there are people who receive the gospel message as
    something other than good news. How might Christians,
    individually and as a church community, have contributed
    to that negative perception of the gospel? What things do
    we say or do which tend to distract from or block God's
    good news of grace, love, forgiveness, and hope?

GROUP DISCOVERY (48 MINUTES)

Video Presentation (20 minutes)

*Watch the video segment for Session 4, using the following outline to
take notes on anything that stands out to you.*

Notes

God's grace — good news that transforms

    Individuals — because God forgives and offers the power to change

Communities—because in crisis we need the support and comfort of God's people

Societies—because even the smallest seed of grace can grow into a great tree

Video Discussion (5 minutes)

He [Jesus] told them another parable: "The kingdom of heaven is like a mustard seed, which a man took and planted in his field. Though it is the smallest of all seeds, yet when it grows, it is the largest of garden plants and becomes a tree, so that the birds come and perch in its branches."

MATTHEW 13:31–32

1. How important is it for people who do not know God to view and receive the message of grace as truly good news? In your own background, did you first encounter the gospel as good news or as something else?

What ideas did you glean from the video about how to build a convincing case (not an argument!) for the gospel actually being good news?

2. Ron Nikkel has seen the good news of God's grace transform prisoners, some of whom people might write off as hopeless. Please share with the group any personal stories of relatives or acquaintances who hit bottom—through crime, addiction, depression—and were transformed by God.

3. What good news of hope and comfort does the community of Jesus-followers have to offer to people who experience tragedy and suffering?

In contrast, what good news do those who deny God's existence have to offer? How might we lovingly share the good news of hope with them?

4. In the parable of the mustard seed (see Matthew 13:31–32 above), what does Jesus indicate about how the transformation of an entire society begins?

What hope does this give each of us for helping even one person to receive the gospel of good news with open hands?

Bible Exploration (18 minutes)

Restoring the Good News of God's Grace

How beautiful on the mountains are the feet of those who bring good news, who proclaim peace, who bring good tidings, who proclaim salvation, who say to Zion, "Your God reigns!"

ISAIAH 52:7

The Christian faith is not simply a private matter to be practiced once a week at church. Rather, it should have a contagious effect on the broader world. Consider what happened in the waning days of the Roman Empire. People flocked to the churches, which stood out as caring communities. A fourth-century Roman emperor known as Julian the Apostate complained bitterly about Christians of his time: "These impious Galileans not only feed their own poor, but ours also ... Whilst the pagan priests neglect the poor, the hated Galileans devote themselves to works of charity."[7] His campaign against the Christians failed, and the gospel continued to spread even as Roman power ebbed. Think of how the good news might permeate our world if we devoted ourselves to conveying the "incomparable riches" of God's grace.

5. Christians in the U.S. today seem to have conveyed to the outside world that the kingdom of God is a set of beliefs and a prescribed standard of behavior, and that the church is a place where like-minded people go to feel better about themselves. This image stands in sharp contrast to the vision of Jesus. He said little about believers' behavior when gathering together and much about how we can positively influence the world—the "outsiders"—around us. In his view, the kingdom of God largely exists for the sake of those outside it, as a tangible expression of God's love for all. Read Matthew 13:31–33 and 5:13–16; as you do, notice the images Jesus uses to illustrate his kingdom and its effects on the broader world.

   • In what ways do these images differ from our tendency to make a big impact with the gospel through citywide campaigns, state or nationwide moral legislation, and the like?

   • What difference do you see between seeking to "paint" a culture Christian and permeating it with the good news of God's grace? What do you see as the short- and long-term outcomes of each approach?

- What specific things do you think we must do in order to have the impact of the mustard seed, yeast, salt, and light in our communities and on our culture? Who is capable of doing this, and why?

6. What evidence do we see that the early Jesus-followers took to heart the transforming power of God's grace and sought to share the good news with thirsty people in their world?

- Acts 9:36; 24:17; Galatians 2:9–10

- Acts 5:12, 15–16; 8:4–8

- Hebrews 13:3

- Hebrews 13:1–2, 16

- Acts 23:11; 26:19–29

7. The New Testament gives little attention to the faults of the surrounding culture. Jesus and Paul say nothing about violent gladiator games or infanticide, both common practices among the Romans. Yet in 1 Corinthians 5:9–13 Paul responds fiercely to a report of incest in the Corinthian church.

- What clear distinction does Paul make about judging moral behavior, and how does it compare to what many people outside the faith have experienced from the Christian community today?

- If the Christian community actually followed Paul's teaching, how might it help to restore the "good news" of the gospel in the minds of people who do not know God?

8. It isn't easy to love God and to express the good news of God's love in a culture that doesn't appreciate it or may even despise it. But God's people and the message of grace have often thrived in such situations.

- How might the perspective we see in God's message to the captured Israelites in Babylon help us to live and dispense grace among the uncommitted in our world? (See Jeremiah 29:4–7.)

- How does Jesus say we are to treat even our enemies, and why (see Luke 6:35 – 36)? If we actually did this, how might it help to restore the "good news" of the gospel in the minds of people who are hostile toward those who proclaim faith in God?

Group Discussion (5 minutes)

God has entrusted flawed human beings with a message so powerful that it sometimes does its work in spite of us. Like a flowing stream, the gospel steadily erodes evil even if the church takes the wrong side — as it sometimes has — and even after a society abandons faith ... Our challenge as Jesus' followers is to align ourselves with the true gospel, and to reclaim the force it has released to a world in desperate need.

VANISHING GRACE, PAGES 170, 171

9. When the Pharisees brought the woman caught in adultery to Jesus (see John 8:3 – 8), they saw two kinds of people: good people like themselves, bad people like her. Jesus also saw two kinds of people: those who needed grace and admitted it, those who needed grace and denied it.

   - Which kinds of people do we tend to see when we look at those outside the faith?

- In what ways does how we view people who do not know God influence our interactions with them, and what impact might our view have on how they receive the good news?

10. Consider the ways those who follow Jesus may minister God's grace to prisoners: visiting and corresponding with them, providing necessities they cannot provide for themselves, caring for their children when they cannot, helping in the difficult task of finding jobs when they are released. It is easy to see why our efforts on their behalf could be received as good news. Now consider the ways we tend to engage the atheist who lives down the street or the lesbian parents of our child's classmate. Is it possible that the gospel message would be received as good news by these people if we extended God's grace to them with the same compassion, love, and care that we extend to those in prison? Explain your answer.

11. People outside the Christian faith who are concerned about the moral decline of our society struggle to answer the question, "How can we get people to be good?" Some of them, including agnostic philosopher Jürgen Habermas, recognize that the Western legacy of conscience, human rights, and democracy "is the direct heir of the Judaic ethic of justice and Christian ethic of love."[8]

- When non-Christians recognize that Christianity has brought some benefit to the world, why do you think it is so difficult for them to look to the Christian community— the bearers of God's good news—for solutions to societal ills that we all agree on?

- Identify several ways that Jesus-followers today can come alongside spiritual outsiders and live out their commitment to the common good—demonstrating in practical ways the moral guidance, values, and hope of the good news?

12. The good news centers on Jesus, who forgave sinners, loved enemies, healed the sick, extended grace to the undeserving, and triumphed as a victim. He demonstrated a different way of being human that truly is good news. What practical ways can you suggest that might help us do a better job of being human in a way that expresses the good news?

PERSONAL REFLECTION (3 MINUTES)

At daybreak, Jesus went out to a solitary place. The people were looking for him and when they came to where he was, they tried to keep him from leaving them. But he said, "I must proclaim the good news of the kingdom of God to the other towns also, because that is why I was sent."

LUKE 4:42–43

Like Jesus, each of us who follow him is also sent to reveal the good news of God's kingdom to a lost world. Unlike Jesus, we sometimes lose our way. We may overlook the fact that much of the good life we have is because of the good news we have been given. We may lose focus on why we are sent. How can we possibly share the good news with thirsty people if we don't fully recognize it as good news ourselves? How can we encourage a robust renewal of faith so that we can demonstrate the truth and power of the good news to a watching world? Perhaps we start by asking ourselves a few questions:

How would your life be different if God had not extended forgiving, life-giving grace to you?

How often do you stop to appreciate what God has done for you?

How can you celebrate the forgiving, life-giving grace God has extended to you, and whom might you invite to celebrate with you?

To what extent do you welcome God's free gift of grace with open hands, turning to God to meet your needs as you go through daily life?

With God's help, what specific things do you do daily to help permeate and season the culture around you with the good news of God's grace?

CLOSING PRAYER (2 MINUTES)

Begin your prayer with these words from the Bible:

> *Whoever does not love does not know God, because God is love. This is how God showed his love among us: He sent his one and only Son into the world that we might live through him. This is love: not that we loved God, but that he loved us and sent his Son as an atoning sacrifice for our sins.*
>
> 1 JOHN 4:8–10

Continue in prayer, humble before God, confessing your shortcomings in living out the good news of God's grace. Thank God for forgiving us, for sending Jesus not only to die for us but to show us a better way of being human. Ask for God's guidance as you grow in grace and seek to demonstrate the good news to a watching, spiritually thirsty world. Pray that you will be grace-filled ambassadors who do God's will on earth as it is done in heaven.

Personal Journey: To Do on Your Own

To the degree we live out the message we say we believe, treating everyone with dignity and worth and measuring success by the standards of Jesus and not the broader culture, to that degree only we will succeed in serving up good news to a thirsty world.

VANISHING GRACE, PAGE 215

Bible Discovery

God's grace benefits everyone. The gospel message provides a foundation for knowing who we are, why we are here, what is good for us, and, most important, who loves us. It is good news indeed— news that gives us a better way to live, a second chance when we fail, hope when we face crisis, and comfort for human suffering.

1. The core of the good news is about God and how God relates to each of us. The Bible reveals the good news about knowing God, loving God, serving God, and living with God in heaven forever.

   Read the following verses: Psalm 100:3; 139:1–4; Isaiah 45:5–6; Jeremiah 31:33–34; John 14:1–3; Ephesians 1:18–21; 5:8–10; Philippians 3:20–21; and 1 Peter 1:3–5. Read with no other goal than to immerse yourself in what the Bible teaches about God and the good news. After you have finished, ask yourself:

   • What does it mean to me that God loves and knows me?

   • When we humans experience God's grace, what deep longings of essential worth, security, and destiny are satisfied?

- Why is this good news for everyone — those who acknowledge God as well as those who do not?

- Why is this good news especially meaningful to me, and how might I sincerely and respectfully share my experience of it with others?

2. Since the first sin in the Garden of Eden, we humans have sought to satisfy our needs and longings in our own ways. And we have become very good at it. Everything our culture offers — wealth, success, fame, security, beauty, power — is a monument to that desire. But the Bible has something to say about the promises of culture. (See Mark 8:36; Luke 12:13 – 15; James 1:10 – 11; 1 John 2:15 – 17.)

- If the best that culture can provide ultimately is bad news, what hope is there for people who do not acknowledge God to find meaning, purpose, and success in life? How might I reach out to nonbelievers I know who struggle with these issues?

- In light of the Bible's perspective on the bad news of culture, how do I show compassion to people who cling desperately to the only hope they know?

- How might this understanding of the deep needs and longings of spiritually lost people motivate me to share God's good news with them more effectively?

Take Action

So many people today choose their own way to live, in effect creating their own "truth" to live by. Without being legalistic, how might you share the good news that following biblical guidelines for life and relationships is beneficial not only for individuals but for communities and society as a whole? Consider the following Bible portions and write out the life principles that benefit everyone.

Bible Passage(s)	Life Principles That Benefit Everyone
1 Corinthians 6:18–20; 7:2; 1 Thessalonians 4:3–4	
Romans 6:11–13	
1 Corinthians 12:21–26	
John 13:12–15	
1 Thessalonians 5:14; James 1:27; Matthew 25:31–45	
1 Corinthians 13:4–7	

What can I do by word and deed to better convey this good news to the people I encounter in my world?

HOLY SUBVERSIVES

Our confused society badly needs a community of contrast, a counterculture of ordinary pilgrims who insist on living a different way… "The world looks with some awe upon a person who appears unconcernedly indifferent to home, money, comfort, rank, or even power and fame," said Winston Churchill. "The world feels not without a certain apprehension, that here is someone outside its jurisdiction; someone before whom its allurements may be spread in vain…"[9] Here is a true subversive.

—*VANISHING GRACE*, PAGES 261, 262

INTRODUCTION (8 MINUTES)

Christians are amphibious creatures, "in the world ... not of the world," in Jesus' words. And in a modern society that runs by competition, self-indulgence, and power, we should stand out because we follow a notably different script. We communicate our faith not by compelling assent but by presenting it as a true answer to spiritual thirst, a shining alternative to evil in the world. That is, in fact, what the early Christians did. They lived by different rules than the surrounding culture, first attracting the attention of outsiders and ultimately winning them over.

Questions to Think About

Choose from among these icebreaker questions as time permits.

1. What would you say are the "rules" of our culture that result in fawning over celebrities and superstar athletes, pitting winners against losers, building bigger houses for smaller families, and achieving success at any cost?

   What do you see as the opposing "subversive" rules of the kingdom of God? (List them!)

2. When a person is described as being "radical," "subversive," "alternative," or "countercultural," what do you think and how do you feel about that person?

What questions do you have about that person and his or her beliefs and motivation?

What kind of relationship do you want with that person? Why?

What insight into how nonbelievers may view you and other Jesus-followers do your answers provide?

3. How comfortable are you with the idea that your personal faith — the way you live every day — is to stand out like a beacon of light in a dark world? Does that intimidate or threaten you? Why?

GROUP DISCOVERY (47 MINUTES)

Video Presentation (20 minutes)

Watch the video segment for Session 5, using the following outline to take notes on anything that stands out to you.

Notes

Big screen versus little screen

Jesus: a call to radical subversion

The Derksens: displaying the path of grace

Live for an audience of One

Video Discussion (5 minutes)

If we live to please God rather than the world around us, if we keep our eyes on that little screen, that's all that matters. If we do it with grace, showing the world a different way to live, the world sits up and takes notice.

FROM THE *VANISHING GRACE* VIDEO

1. How does the "big screen, little screen" imagery help you to understand the role of the church — the community of Christians — in culture?

   Why do you think the church leans toward stepping into the "big screen" role, and what happens when it does?

   How difficult is it for us to focus on the "little screen" when what's playing on the big screen flashes its message in HD, with action-packed special effects, at top volume?

2. When renowned writer Malcolm Gladwell encountered the Derksens, it changed him forever. As you watched the Derksen interview, what "little screen" message stood out to you, and what impact does it have on you?

3. What do you think it might look like if a person lived for an audience of One in our culture?

How do you think our involvement in culture and inter-action with non-Christians would change if we lived only for an audience of One?

What personal price might we pay to live for an audience of One?

4. Why do you think a radical but grace-filled faith in Jesus communicates so powerfully to spiritually thirsty people?

In what ways do you find actually living out that faith easy or difficult?

Bible Exploration (15 minutes)

Lessons in Grace-Filled Subversion

The devil led him [Jesus] up to a high place and showed him in an instant all the kingdoms of the world. And he said to him, "I will give you all their authority and splendor; it has been given to me, and I can give it to anyone I want to. If you worship me, it will all be yours." Jesus answered, "It is written: 'Worship the Lord your God and serve him only.'"

LUKE 4:5 – 8

Jesus is our example of how to live according to the priorities of God's kingdom instead of those of this world. In so doing, he modeled for us a new way to be human. He has shown us the way to live with the goal of pleasing God, not just to feed our egos, achieve success, and rise in prestige. He calls us to see the same worth in a homeless person as in a billionaire; to devote attention to the sick and weak, not just the glamorous and beautiful; to love all people through the power of his grace.

5. The message of Jesus plays out on the "little screen," a radical subversion of what is featured on the "big screen." Together, read aloud the Beatitudes, recorded in Matthew 5:1 – 11.

• Although in this teaching Jesus doesn't advocate taking direct actions to oppose the culture, in what ways does it subvert, or turn upside down, some of the cherished values of the world? In other words, how do the Beatitudes contradict the message of the "big screen"?

'planting'
The 'Culture

- Talk about practical ways we might demonstrate this teaching in our culture.

Bush 41
Funeral

6. Let's also consider occasions when Jesus was more overt in opposing the established powers. What establishment-shattering messages did Jesus send in Matthew 21:12–13; 27:62–28:6? *drove out money changes*
resurrection

no fear of death / women as witness

Jesus could have taken in-your-face actions such as these many times during his ministry, yet he did not. What do you think motivated him to take these particular actions, and what was his purpose for doing so?

As Jesus-followers who want to express God's good news, we need to know when to demonstrate subversive values by how we live and when to take overt action. What do you learn from these examples about when it may be appropriate to take confrontational action?

7. Having personally demonstrated the good news of God's
grace on earth, Jesus is well aware of what we will face as
grace-filled subversives. He warned his disciples that a hostile
reception should neither surprise nor deter them, saying
"Go! I am sending you out like lambs among wolves!" (Luke
10:3). It is no different for his followers today. What reassur-
ance, instruction, and advice does Jesus offer in each of the
following passages? How will his words help us to be more
faithful in extending God's grace to spiritually thirsty people?

- Matthew 6:19–21 *Sermon on the Mount*
retirement savings in heaven

- Matthew 6:25–26 *daily care*

- Matthew 7:13–14 *narrow gate*

- Luke 6:27–31 *not to worry*
to seek God's kingdom

- Luke 14:33–35 *cost of discipleship*

8. Each of us is imperfect and fallible. Although we intend to share the good news, it is all too easy for us to get caught up in appearances and results and start doing God's work according to the priorities and methods of the very culture we want to influence.

- What overarching priority did Jesus follow that can also keep us on track as messengers of God's good news? (See John 4:34; 5:30.) *"my food is to do The will of the one who sent me"* *"I seek not to please myself"*

- What does Jesus teach us that will help us to keep our focus on pleasing God above all else? (See Matthew 22:37; 6:33; John 14:15.) *J14 "If you love me you'll obey ___ what I command* *M6:33 Seek first the kingdom* *M22:32 - Love the Lord your God with all your heart soul and mind*

9. What do the following verses reveal about what is required of those who are serious about living for an audience of One? (See 1 Corinthians 9:24–27; Colossians 3:23–24; 2 Timothy 4:6–8; Hebrews 12:1–3.)
Run the race to win. *Work as to the Lord, not as to men* *fight the good fight* *Run the race fixed on Jesus*

Group Discussion (7 minutes)

A post-Christian society is quick to remind us of our faults, which we should humbly acknowledge. Yet wherever the gospel has taken root, it has borne fruit. Much that we value in the modern world — freedom, democracy, education, healthcare, human rights, social justice—traces back to a Christian origin... "The personal religious convictions of individuals," says British historian Paul Johnson, "gradually and necessarily permeate society by persuasion and example."[10] The smallest seed in the garden has become a great tree in which the birds of the air come to nest.

VANISHING GRACE, PAGES 270, 259

10. History shows that the Christian faith grows best from the bottom up rather than being imposed from the top down. As Miroslav Volf observes, "Imposition stands starkly at odds with the basic character of the Christian faith, which is at heart about self-giving—God's self-giving and human self-giving—and not about self-imposing."[11]

   • How do Jesus-followers today permeate and influence society with the good news by being subversive but not coercive, self-giving but not self-imposing?

   To compell by force or intimidation subvert — to overthrow something established or existing, undermine the principals —

   • What is the difference in motivation and action between being subversive and being coercive? Why is it important that we know the difference and live accordingly?

11. What steps must we, as individuals and as the church, take to keep the broader culture from determining our values and measures of success?

Which core truths must we live by if we are to demonstrate Jesus' radical way of dispensing grace?

12. We live in an increasingly postmodern culture that is moving away from any absolute moral code. In such a world, why is it essential that Christians listen well, live well, and engage well if we are to play a role in bringing biblical clarity to moral issues?

much discerned ! !

How well do you think the Christian community presents moral truth without casting judgments on others, and how might we do better?

What ways can you think of to present moral truth with grace in a culture that quickly labels anyone who takes a moral stand as being "intolerant"?

When we encounter people who oppose any absolute moral code, yet act "from habits of the heart" and make moral choices that are rooted primarily in our Christian heritage, how might we forge grace-filled connections with them that give us opportunities to share the good news?

PERSONAL REFLECTION (3 MINUTES)

Christ-followers need not live in fear, even when it seems that society may be turning against us. We rest in full confidence that God, in control of human history, will have the final word: "The kingdom of the world has become the kingdom of our Lord and of his Messiah, and he will reign for ever and ever." We each of us do our part, loving others as God loves us, tending the world as stewards of a gracious landlord. The yeast spreads, the salt preserves, the tree survives, even in dark and foreboding times.

VANISHING GRACE, PAGE 270

As dispensers of God's grace, we are not responsible for the end result; that lies safely, incorruptibly in God's hands. We are responsible to do our part to the best of our ability and with all the strength, wisdom, and grace God provides for us. Each of us can live a grace-filled life, and together we can be a community of subversives, displaying in the "little screen" a contrasting view of life, an image of what God's kingdom looks like.

When has the "little screen" message of Jesus' way grabbed your attention and made a difference in your life?

What about the message and the person presenting it caught your attention?

What "little screen" message(s) has God given you to share with a watching world?

What steps do you take to ensure that you share this message with God's grace, as Paul writes, "always full of grace, seasoned with salt" (Colossians 4:6) and nothing more?

How prepared are you to share this message whenever an opportunity presents itself?

CLOSING PRAYER (2 MINUTES)

Begin your prayer with these words from the Bible:

> *The appeal we make does not spring from error or*
> *impure motives, nor are we trying to trick you. On*
> *the contrary, we speak as those approved by God to be*
> *entrusted with the gospel. We are not trying to please*
> *people but God, who tests our hearts. You know we*
> *never used flattery, nor did we put on a mask to cover*
> *up greed — God is our witness. We were not looking for*
> *praise from people, not from you or anyone else.*
>
> 1 THESSALONIANS 2:3–6

Continue in prayer, asking God to keep your focus clear and your hearts pure as you seek to share the life-changing good news of the gospel. Pray that you will not become enamored by the allure of the "big screen," but will be content and at peace, faithfully living out your faith for an audience of One — the only audience that really matters. Express your desire as subversive pilgrims, activists, and artists to take what you've learned to heart and pour out God's grace in a way that will turn a thirsty world upside down.

Personal Journey: To Do on Your Own

*Brothers and sisters, think of what you were when you
were called. Not many of you were wise by human
standards; not many were influential; not many were
of noble birth. But God chose the foolish things of the
world to shame the wise; God chose the weak things
of the world to shame the strong. God chose the lowly
things of this world and the despised things—and the
things that are not—to nullify the things that are, so
that no one may boast before him.*

1 CORINTHIANS 1:26–29

Bible Discovery

Every Christian can be an activist, whether full- or part-time. Out
of the media spotlight, we act out our beliefs. Against the grain of
surrounding culture we find creative ways to fight moral battles.
When parents discard unwanted children, Christians make a home
for them. When scientists seek ways to purify the gene pool, Christians look for special-needs babies to adopt. When politicians cut
funding for the poor, Christians open shelters and feeding stations.
When law enforcement confines criminals behind barbed wire,
Christians run programs for them. As holy subversives, we permeate our culture with God's grace and reveal an alternative way to live,
a different way to be human.

1. Jesus-followers today are very much in the world. We know
   how the world works and how to get what we want in it. So
   it's a radical change to live as Jesus lived, to learn a different
   way of being human. In the following Bible passages, Jesus
   interacts with the powers of the earthly kingdom. Notice
   how he demonstrates a different way to be human.

- Matthew 4:8–10: Our natural, human inclination is to use and benefit from what the kingdom of this world offers. How do we know when we need to turn away from it, even when it may seem to serve us well?

- Matthew 22:15–21: In this world, whoever grasps the greatest power wins. What do we gain when we sidestep the power struggle and focus on what is most important?

- Matthew 26:45–54: Self-preservation is necessary for success in the world's kingdom. What is the greater purpose that enables a person who knows God to lay down his or her life?

2. Today many Christians try to exert political power in order to provide moral guidance and influence culture. This has certainly contributed to the "anti-this, anti-that" reputation that many post- and non-Christians attribute to Christians. Given what you have discussed in the *Vanishing Grace* study, consider how followers of Jesus might influence our culture through politics in a way that does not drown out our core message of love and grace. Identify the advantages and disadvantages of the following possible approaches:

- Completely withdraw from the political process.

- Engage in the political process—and choose which injustices to fight and when to compromise on issues even when we disagree with people's positions.

- Enforce our beliefs and values, even on those who do not share them—in order to change the world for Christ.

- Form alliances with other religious groups in areas of mutual concern and shared moral vision in order to bring about change.

- Distinguish between what is illegal and immoral, and not try to impose our moral code on non-Christians through law.

- Align cautiously with the state—in order to remain effective in challenging surrounding culture.

Take Action

As you conclude this study, remember that God has chosen us not because we are wise or influential, not because we are strong or respected, but because we have accepted the good news of God's gift of forgiveness and grace. Whatever our calling—pilgrim, activist, or artist—we are joined together to proclaim with joy and grace God's good news to the world. Consider how God might be calling you to operate as a holy subversive within the broader culture. Then write down how and what you will start communicating through the "little screen."

Calling	Opportunities to Be a Holy Subversive	The Message I Proclaim Via the "Little Screen"
Pilgrims		
"Ordinary" Christians acting in love who reflect Jesus, acknowledge their "lostness" and moral inferiority, and desire God's help in finding the way.	Choose to forgive, not act with rage and revenge; lavish attention on the least "deserving"; be unconcernedly indifferent to money, comfort, rank, power, fame; bear the good news in humility; admit need of God for vision and strength to subvert the world.	

Calling	Opportunities to Be a Holy Subversive	The Message I Proclaim Via the "Little Screen"
Activists		
Christians who act out in love as the hands and feet of Jesus to address injustices and unmet human needs, as well as those who pray for and support those who undertake such actions; go against the grain of surrounding culture in grace-full ways that may challenge even corrupt institutions.	Pray, volunteer, and/or contribute financially; help needy people; care for weak and dis-advantaged; reach out to prisoners; intervene in sexual trafficking; relieve the oppressed; face institutional corruption. May engage in civil dis-obedience or act to gain the attention of a numb society.	
Artists		
Christians who use art, including writing, to communi-cate something the viewer, listener, or reader knows yet doesn't recognize in order to create new awareness.	Draw readers, observers, or listeners into the Christian artist's attitudes, feel-ings, and total experiences—i.e., an article, book, poem, or blog; painting; music; drama; sculpture. Connect with receivers' issues, emotions, intel-lect in stimulating ways that exhibit grace.	

NOTES

1. Quoted from David Kinnaman and Gabe Lyons, *UnChristian: What a New Generation Really Thinks about Christianity ... and Why It Matters* (Grand Rapids: Baker, 2007), 26.

2. Theodore Dalrymple, "What the New Atheists Don't See," *City Journal* (Autumn 2007): city-journal.org/html/17_4_oh_to_be.html.

3. Harper Lee, *To Kill a Mockingbird* (New York: Popular Library, 1962), 34.

4. Barbara Brown Taylor, *An Altar in the World: A Geography of Faith* (New York: HarperOne, 2009), 72–73.

5. Thanks to Kathryn Helmers for this insight.

6. Rick Warren, quoted in James Davison Hunter, *To Change the World: The Irony, Tragedy, and Possibility of Christianity in the Late Modern World* (New York: Oxford University Press, 2010), 221.

7. Quoted in James Davison Hunter, *To Change the World: The Irony, Tragedy, and Possibility of Christianity in the Late Modern World*, 55–56.

8. Jürgen Habermas, *The Habermas Forum* (May 3, 2009): http://www.habermasforum.dk/index.php?type=news&text_id=451.

9. Winston Churchill, *Never Give In!: The Best of Winston Churchill's Speeches* (New York: Hyperion, 2003), 139–140.

10. Paul Johnson, *A History of Christianity* (New York: Atheneum, 1976), 429.

11. Miroslav Volf, *A Public Faith: How Followers of Christ Should Serve the Common Good* (Grand Rapids: Brazos, 2011), 106.

Vanishing Grace

Whatever Happened to the Good News?

Philip Yancey

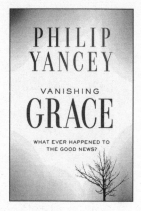

Why does the church stir up such negative feelings?

Philip Yancey has been asking this all his life as a journalist. His perennial question is more relevant now than ever. Research shows that favorable opinions of Christianity have plummeted drastically—and opinions of Evangelicals have taken even deeper dives.

So what's so good about the "Good News"?

In his landmark book, *What's So Amazing about Grace*, Yancey issued a call for Christians to be as grace-filled in their behavior as they are in declaring their beliefs. He now aims this book at Christians again, showing them how they have lost respect, influence, and reputation in a newly post-Christian culture. Exploring what may have contributed to hostility toward Evangelicals—especially in their mixing of faith and politics instead of embracing more grace-filled ways of presenting the gospel—Yancey offers illuminating stories of how faith can be expressed in ways that disarm even the most cynical critics. Then he explores what is Good News and what is worth preserving in a culture that thinks it has rejected Christian faith.

Available in stores and online!